The Fonners of Fonner Run

In Morris Township, Greene County, Pennsylvania

By

D. Kent Fonner

Westlake, Ohio

THE FONNERS OF FONNER RUN: IN MORRIS TOWNSHIP, GREENE COUNTY, PENNSYLVANIA

Printed in the United States of America

ISBN 9798698768760

Front cover is a photograph of the Fred Fonner farm with Fred and his son, Albert, sitting on the stone step, flanked by Fred's daughters, Emma and Myrtle. In back of them are his daughters, Mary and Jessie. The other man in the picture is an unidentified hired hand. Back cover is a photograph of Henry B. Fonner throwing hay in the barn sometime after he returned home from the army.

Henry B. Fonner and Helen (Jacobs) Fonner
March 1944

PREFACE

The purpose of this book is to make a more permanent record of my researches in the Fonner family history. Years ago, my cousin, Emma (Babe) Hoge, told me that her aunts, Myrtle and Emma Fonner, one day had her brother, Luther Thompson, take a trunk full of "old papers" belonging to their father, Fred Fonner, outside and burn it. Another relative, one of my aunts, decided to remove genealogical record pages from the Fonner family Bible. Accordingly, much history was lost. Public records, however, and publications by related family genealogists, such as Dorothy Hennen, have preserved a great deal of the story. I hope this work will give future generations a place to start their own investigations. I make no pretense that this is definitive. I have also limited this work to the ancestors of my direct line. There are several branches of Fonners living in the United States. It is likely we are all related to common immigrant ancestors. I therefore ask your indulgence as you peruse this work. It remains a labor of love dedicated to my parents, Henry B. Fonner and Helen (Jacobs) Fonner, and my five siblings.

16 October 2020   D. Kent Fonner

Henry B. Fonner and Helen (Jacobs) Fonner
On the day of their engagement, 1943

CHAPTER I
Henry B. Fonner, Citizen Soldier in World War II

My brother-in-law, James Flanigan, and my sister, Ellen, were sitting in the living room one Sunday afternoon watching a movie on TV. My father, Henry B. Fonner, came through the room and Jim invited him to sit and watch the show. He explained to Dad that the movie was about the Battle of the Bulge. Dad looked at him and simply replied, "No thanks! I was in the play!"

That exchange was probably about as much as he ever said to us Fonner children about his experiences in World War II. Sometimes, if we were watching a movie or TV show, like the old 1960s series, "Combat," he would slip out a word or two, but he did not like to talk about it, and we all respected his privacy. Once, my brother, Albert, was reading a book on the Battle of the Bulge, *A Time for Trumpets* by Charles MacDonald. The book mentions Tech Sergeant Fred Wallace of Company E of the 394th Infantry, 99th Division. We later learned that Sergeant Wallace had been Dad's platoon sergeant (the 3rd Platoon of Company E). Albert asked him if he remembered Wallace, and Dad just snickered, and said he remembered him. Albert did not pursue the question any further.

When Dad came home from Europe on a hot summer day in 1945, he got off a bus from Pittsburgh at the corner of High and Washington streets in Waynesburg and walked down the hill to First Street to the home of my grandparents, J. Warren and Emma Jacobs. My sister Ann had been born in May, and mom was staying at their house. No one knew he was coming home that day, so no one met him at the bus stop. As he walked down the street in his uniform, Grandma Jacobs saw him. By the time he reached the house, he was greeted by mom holding Ann in her arms. That was the first time he saw his first child, and the beginning of his post-war life in Greene County.

No doubt his experiences were typical of many Greene County men and boys in the 1940s. Although the statistics are not certain, there is evidence that over five thousand Greene County men and women served in the United States military during World War II. In their final report after the war, the county's two draft boards noted that 4700 draftees had been inducted from Greene County. In addition, at least 435 men and women volunteered for service in the armed forces. When he was sent to Europe with the 99th Division in the Fall of 1944, Dad was thirty-one years old. Another Company E veteran, Curtis Whiteway, author of a book titled, *Brave Men Don't Cry,* told me in a letter that since most of the "men" in the "company were eighteen, nineteen, and twenty year-olds, Dad must have been one of the oldest infantrymen in the outfit. Whiteway was in a different platoon and did not know him, but he said they had a thirty-something year-old man in his infantry squad who was just not able to keep up with the kids. Eventually, he was assigned to headquarters as a jeep driver. Dad, however, being raised on a Greene County farm on Fonner Run in Morris Township, stayed with his infantry squad throughout training and right up to service on the front line in the Ardennes Forest of Belgium.

I

Henry B. Fonner was born on his parents' farm in Morris Township, Greene County, Pennsylvania, on 18 May 1913. His father, Albert Edward Fonner, was a tall, strong, farmer of Pennsylvania Dutch ancestry. His father, Fred Fonner, who was married to Eleanor Penn, was the son of James Fonner, always referred to by the family as "the Old Dutchman." James was just a boy when he migrated to Greene County with his father, William Fonner, and the rest of his relatives, from Bloom Township, Northumberland County, Pennsylvania, in 1804. William eventually purchased the family a large farm in Morris Township in 1820. The Albert Fonner family lived on a farm of about ninety acres of the original tract, which had once included several hundred acres of the valley, or hollow, now known as Fonner Run. Henry's mother, Annie Simpson Fonner, was a slightly-framed woman of Irish descent. Her father, Hugh Simpson, had a large farm on what is now called Simpson Ridge in Morris Township, just across the bridge and up the hill from the old Swarts Church. As a matter of fact, Annie's great-grandfather, Reverend John Simpson, was a Methodist preacher who emigrated from Ireland in the 1790s and established a Methodist meeting place on his farm above present day Swarts. That meeting place eventually led to the building of Simpson's Chapel and the dedication of a Methodist cemetery part-way up Simpson Ridge from Swarts. When the W and W RR was built, and Swarts Station was established in the village once known as Hopkins Mill, the Simpson Chapel was moved down to its present location in Swarts and served as a Methodist Church from the 1870s until it was closed by the Conference in 1996. Henry inherited his mother's short stature, but as he grew on the farm, he developed a powerful, muscular, body that served him well during his time in the army.

Like many Greene County boys at the time, Henry learned farming from the ground up. He became expert with a team of Belgians in the garden, corn fields, and hay fields around the farm. While many Greene County farms had sheep, a severe case of foot rot made the Albert Fonner farm unhealthy for sheep, so the bottom pasture was the domain of a herd of milk cows. In the meantime, the Old Sheep Shed, scene of a Civil War era family legend, fell into disrepair and eventually collapsed. The Fonner farm was a hardscrabble place with only one "bottom" pasture and the rest of the 90 acres on hills. They had six or eight dairy cows, chickens, pigs, and a team of horses. His life was a cycle of plowing, planting, cultivating, harvesting, and haying, as well as milking the cows and caring for the livestock. During times of relaxation, he and his father would sit on the porch and play music. He was talented with the fiddle and the banjo.

His older sisters, Grace Rinehart and Goldie Auld, remembered the farm as a "showplace" when they were young girls and women. Goldie lived in the tenant house on the farm and was widowed when her husband died in a farming accident.

She gave birth to a son, Robert Auld, at about the same time Henry was born. The two boys grew up together and shared many adventures on the farm. It was Goldie who supplied the boys with a hunting rifle, and on their trips into the woods, Henry developed into an expert marksman. They attended school at the Fonner Schoolhouse, a one-room school located on the far edge of the hayfield just above the public road leading to the farm. In addition, Henry also attended the Morris Township High School in Nineveh. As an older teenager, however, Henry was the last of the Fonner boys at home on the farm. He became more involved with operating the farm on a daily basis, and his education ended after two years of high school.

It was his farm responsibilities, however, that also led to his marriage to his wife, Helen Mae Jacobs, the youngest daughter of J. Warren Jacobs, Greene County's noted ornithologist, oologist, and birdhouse manufacturer. Helen worked as a secretary and cream tester at the Fairmount Creamery in Waynesburg on First Street. The creamery was managed by her brother, Bryan Jacobs. She told the story that Henry would bring milk in from the farm every Saturday and always spend a little extra time talking with her in the office. He wore his best clothes and always had a bright new shine on his shoes. There was a railing in front of her desk, and she said he often would put his foot on the railing while they talked so she got a good look at his shoes. They soon started dating in the early 1940s and became engaged while he was home on his first leave from the army on 18 May 1943. They told her father while he was working in his wildflower garden on the north bank of Ten Mile Creek at the foot of Washington Street, and he took their picture while they stood together in the garden.

II

Henry Fonner was drafted into the army in November 1942. He left Waynesburg with a batch of draftees by bus to Pittsburgh and was inducted into the army on 2 December 1942. The War Department was forming a new division, the 99th, which was originally intended as a sister division to

Pennsylvania's 28th Division. At the 99th Division's training camp, Camp Van Dorn, in Mississippi, Fonner was assigned as a rifleman in Company E, 394th U.S. Infantry Regiment. He was placed in the 3rd Platoon of the company under Tech Sergeant Fred Wallace and Lt. William Huttinger. Fonner remembered after the war that the lieutenant commanding the platoon had been a medical student before he was taken from school and assigned an infantry command. The 99th Division was composed of three infantry regiments. These were the 393rd, the 394th, and the 395th Infantry. Company E was in the 2nd Battalion of the 394th Infantry. The Company was divided into three platoons of riflemen, about forty men to each platoon, and a fourth platoon composed of special weapons such as mortars. The platoon was broken down into three squads of twelve men each commanded by a buck sergeant. Fonner's squad leader was a young man from Houtzdale, Pennsylvania, Luther Baughman. The two men became good friends and Baughman visited Fonner several times at his home in Greene County after the war. Other men in the squad included Corporal Vincent White, from central Pennsylvania, Johnny Ryan, a "big burley Irishman," from Philadelphia, Cecil Hetrick, another Pennsylvania man, Irwin Kessler from Ohio, Paul Sandridge, from "old Virginny," a New Yorker named Shuster, two men from Tennessee named Pierce and Shirl, and two other men whose names Fonner forgot. Camp Van Dorn remained his home in the army for about ten months until field maneuvers ended with the regiment and the rest of the 99th Division at Camp Maxey near Paris, Texas, a little less than a hundred miles from Texarkana. There the men received advanced combat training and additional recruits from throughout the United States to help fill the ranks to full capacity. Many of these young men had been college students attending school under the Army Specialized Training Program (ASTP). Now they found themselves with rifles instead of books, and their education placed on hold. Among the new men brought into Company E was Curt Whiteway from Massachusetts, who had been in army ranger training prior to his assignment with the infantry.

At Camp Van Dorn, in addition to his duties as a

rifleman, Fonner assisted in training other men in the use of the rifle. He never achieved rank above private first class because he tended to stutter when he talked, but his expert marksmanship was placed to good use in teaching others how to shoot. He was also given the job of company barber.   A.J. Spinato, a member of the fourth platoon mortar squad, remembered the day that Fonner was assigned the job of company barber. Company E was standing in formation and Captain William Patterson, company commander, was present. Spinato told the story:

> I remember the dread one day when in formation Capt. Pat walked down the line and when he reached Fonner, stopped, handing him a package, saying, "you are the company barber" . . . I hated the thought of an amateur cutting my hair. Maybe Fonner was a barber by trade, because he got to be damn good . . . . I do, however remember apprehensively sitting while he unrolled the [tools] of trade."

To Spinato, Fonner appeared to be a "sort of quiet, soft speaking man." He was "a good listener, and I would relax, relate my fears and trepidations as he cut my hair." Captain Patterson liked him very much. He joked around a lot with Hank, as he was called by the men in the company, and the captain bragged to the Battalion staff that E company had the best barber in the outfit. In addition to the enlisted men and officers in Company E, Fonner cut the hair of all the Battalion staff, including the Battalion Commander, Colonel Olmstead. After the war, Captain Patterson wrote that Henry Fonner "performed all of his duties in a commendable manner. His pleasing personality, cooperative spirit and willingness to do his best at any duties assigned him, led to a perfect record." Moreover, Patterson believed that Fonner "performed his duties as a barber and as a soldier in a superior manner." He stated that Fonner's "character and conduct were unquestionable."

Of course his duties as a barber did not take him away from important duties also as a rifleman on the front line. Spinato remembered that Fonner's platoon Sergeant, Fred

Wallace, was " the best soldier in E company." He further remembered that "from the first day the third platoon got the dangerous patrols and assignments, because of Sergeant Wallace. Pat went to his strength in assigning duties." Though Spinato was in the fourth platoon he knew many of the men in the third platoon including Fonner's squad leader, Sergeant Baughman. During the Battle the Bulge in December 1944, Spinato noted that company E "was in it thick" and "the third platoon was our best. I can also say that Baughman's squad was one they relied on for the tough jobs." He noted that Baughman was a "great soldier" and led several patrols during the Bulge. Spinato further stated that Baughman was "levelheaded, cautious and smart. He was a good leader to follow."

It is clear, therefore, that Fonner, in addition to his duties as a barber, also was involved in heavy combat once his outfit was posted overseas on the front line in Belgium. During his first leave from the Army in May 1943, he became engaged to his future wife, Helen Mae Fonner. The next year, on a second leave from the Army, the couple became married on 21 March 1944 in a simple ceremony held at the parsonage of the Nineveh Methodist Church. He returned on leave one more time before going overseas in July 1944 after his father, Albert Fonner, died. His mother, Annie, had died when he was still a young man living on the farm in 1940. After he was drafted into the Army, his father became convinced that Henry would not come back from the war alive and so he simply gave up any will to live. He did not want to outlive his son, and when he became sick that summer he simply refused any treatment. After their marriage, Helen lived for a time in a boarding house in Paris, Texas, where she could be close to her new husband and they could spend some time together before he was sent on active duty to Europe. When the 99th division was sent overseas that fall, she was pregnant with their first child, Ann, who was born in May 1945.

III

The 99th division, including the 394th infantry was sent

to Europe in the fall of 1944. The regiment along with the other units of the 99th division made its way across the country by railroad from Texas to Camp Myles Standish outside Boston in Massachusetts. At Boston the men boarded their transport ships to make a long convoy trip across the ocean to Scotland and England. The 2nd Battalion of the 394th Infantry, including company E, was transported on a ship named "The Exchequer." Fonner remembered the trip as long and sickening. He suffered seasickness the whole way across as the "Exchequer" zigzagged across the Atlantic, to avoid German U-boats. During the trip, the men on board the ship awoke one day to find "The Exchequer" surrounded by a tight circle of Navy destroyers who were firing their guns and dropping depth charges. The men thought they were witnessing a drill, and only later found out that the ship had been under attack by a German U-boat. Eventually, "The Exchequer" and its cargo made landfall at Glasgow, Scotland. After the men were landed from the ship, they boarded a night train which took them to their base camp in southern England. After some additional training in southern England, the 99th division was placed on ships and sent to France, across the English Channel.

On 3 November 1944, Company E found itself just behind the front line in Belgium preparing to relieve units of the 60th infantry Regiment of the 9th infantry division. The day was freezing cold and rainy as the men marched through the woods with full duffel bags and huge horseshoe packs. This was equipment they had brought with them from Camp Maxey in Texas. When they arrived at their dispersion point, the men were ordered to drop their duffel bags and packs, taking only their great coats. So wearing olive drab uniforms, summer underwear and socks, desert shoes, and greatcoat, with a rifle and one belt of ammunition and old type small shovels or picks, they went onto line. They never again saw their duffel bags or the winter clothing that they held. From that point, the company was on the front, opposing the German army in the dense forests, starting their work as combat infantrymen.

The 99th division was placed in the line to relieve the 9th division for other duties. The division held a position along the International Highway which separates Belgium and Germany from a town in the south known as Losheimergraben with a small Intelligence and Reconnaisance platoon covering the village of Lanzareth up to and including the town of Monschau in the north. The 394th infantry Regiment was assigned the position on the South from Lanzerath to the intersection where the road from the German village of Neuhof connects with the International Highway. The second Battalion held the most northern section of the regiment's front in the Honsfelder Wald of the Ardennes Forest, with E company on the extreme northern, left flank, anchored at the intersection where the road from Neuhof joined the International Highway. A single logging trail road connected the battalion to regimental headquarters at the Belgian town of Murringen. North of E company's position began the positions of the 393rd Infantry. For the next month, the men went on patrols and held the line, living in foxholes that had originally been dug by the 9th infantry division. It was cold, wet, muddy work and, because of the lack of winter equipment, other than great coats, many men on the front lines soon began to suffer from illness and frozen feet. Curt Whiteway remembered that when he was coming back from a patrol, he began stumbling and could not hold onto his rifle. It was determined that his feet and hands were both frozen to a point where he had to be taken off the line and sent to a hospital in the rear. The same conditions were suffered by other men all along the line.

After the war, Fonner often talked to his wife, Helen, about the wonderful Irish tenor in his squad, named Johnny Ryan. He also often talked of wanting to go to Philadelphia to look up Johnny Ryan's mother. She said she asked him once whatever happened to Johnny Ryan. He said he did not know. It was not until a visit by Luther Baughman that she found out part of the story. In a letter to Henry, Baughman had said, "It was a shame about what happened to Johnny Ryan." It was forty years after the war before her husband told her the whole story.

On 16 December 1944, the opening day of the Battle of the Bulge, Fonner and his squad, led by Sergeant Luther

Baughman, were stationed somewhere near the crossroads of the International Highway and the road from Neuhof in the woods on the northern flank of the 394th Infantry. Baughman remembered that when the battle began on the 16th, he and Fonner, along with other squad members, Johnny Ryan and Cpl. Vincent White, were holding an isolated outpost. Early that morning, the German bombardment began in preparation for the advancing infantry and armored divisions. The Bulge developed eventually into the largest land battle fought by the United States Army and witnessed some of the worst fighting of the European theater. As German units of the 277th Volksgrenadiers approached the American positions near the road intersection, they began infiltrating within the foxhole line being held by E Company. As the Germans came closer, Sergeant Wallace, knowing his men were sheltered in covered foxholes, called down an artillery barrage on his platoon's isolated position which caught the Germans by surprise. One Company E man, using a Browning Automatic Rifle (BAR) climbed on the roof of a log shelter and sprayed the advancing grenadiers with rounds from the BAR, driving them back down the road toward Neuhof. Another Company E man broke an assault on the foxhole line by firing nearly simultaneous mortar rounds at an infiltrating German patrol and a column of half-tracks.

At one point, Baughman told Helen, Fonner became separated from the squad when he picked up Johnny Ryan, who had his legs blown off when an artillery shell struck a nearby tree. Baughman stated that the last time he saw Henry that day, he was carrying Ryan to an aid station. Forty years later, Fonner related to his wife how Ryan died in his arms after he had carried him approximately a half mile to the rear. Doing what he was trained to do, he laid Ryan on the ground, covering his body so it could later be found by a burial team. Ryan's body was eventually recovered, and he is interred in the Henri-Chapelle American Cemetery near Hombourg, Belgium,

By the time Ryan died, however, Fonner had become

Henry B. Fonner, 99th Division

Henry B. Fonner at Camp Van Dorn, Mississippi

disoriented in the thick pine forest and was lost behind the advancing German lines. Eventually three Belgian girls found him lying unconscious along a forest road. They took him to their home where they hid him in the cellar with three other allied soldiers. As the Germans continued to advance, they kept him safe for four days until it was possible for him and his comrades to try to make their way back to the American lines established on Elsenborn Ridge by the survivors of the 99th division. Of the four men who left that Belgian family, two made it back to the American lines. Fonner, subject to a Christmas miracle, arrived in Elsenborn on Christmas Eve. By the time he got back to the American side of the field, however, his feet had become frozen and the doctors had to cut his shoes off. He had amnesia for several weeks afterwards and was transferred to various hospitals in France before he finally was assigned to a reinforcement battalion and given duty guarding German POWs. His feet bothered him for the rest of his life. He took special care of them on a daily basis and was granted a fifty per cent disability by the Veterans Administration.

At one point, when Fonner was in the hospital near LaHarve in France, his brother-in-law, Al Allison, who was in the Navy, was stationed only a few miles away. Al never knew that he was that close to Fonner, and so he never got the opportunity to visit him in the hospital. As he moved from hospital to hospital Fonner was able to maintain his gear with him, including his helmet. The helmet had two holes in it where a bullet had entered and ricocheted off the liner. He held onto the helmet the whole time until the last hospital, where someone relieved him of the souvenir. He was sent back to the states on 28 May 1945, arriving on 16 June 1945. Granted an honorable discharge, he was separated from the army and returned to civilian life from the Hospital Center at Camp Pickett, Virginia.

While in the service, Fonner suffered two wounds. During a training exercise in the states, he tripped and fell on his own bayonet, cutting his lip. The second wound was a split knuckle. Fonner related that guarding German POW work details was easier when the POWs were older men. Younger

Germans, however, proved harder to handle. One day, while guarding a work detail, Fonner directed a young German POW to do some job, and the young man proceeded to spout off in German in a hostile tone. Fonner did not speak German, but he perfectly understood that he was being cursed. Drawing back his fist, he sent the young man flying backwards with a broken jaw. He carried the scar from the split knuckle for the rest of his life.

IV

After Henry came home from Europe, he lived nearly another fifty years. He and his wife, Helen, celebrated their fiftieth wedding anniversary in 1994. They could look back and remember the six children they raised and celebrate their grandchildren. He continued to farm after the war on the Fonner family farm in Morris Township. He also worked twenty-five years as a warehouseman and laborer at the Jacobs Oil Products warehouse and bulk plant at the foot of Washington Street in Waynesburg. He could often be seen in the bulk plant on top of a tank truck loading heating oil and gasoline for delivery to Jacobs' customers. Despite his silence on the matter, however, his experiences in the army never strayed far from his memory. Helen told the story that one time, shortly after they moved on the farm, she was in the house watching him carry two buckets of milk from the barn to the house. As he was in the middle of the dirt road in front of the barn, there was a gunshot, no doubt from a neighbor out hunting in some nearby woods. Henry immediately threw both buckets of milk in the air and hit the ground flat in the dirt in the middle of the road. He looked around, chuckled to himself, and got back up off the ground, retrieved the empty pails, and proceeded to the house. At other times, she noted, he would wake up in the middle of the night during a thunderstorm, shaking from a flashback to the sounds of the German bombardment at the Bulge.

He was not a member of the VFW or the American Legion until late in life. His old squad leader, Luther Baughman, came to Greene County from Houtzdale,

Pennsylvania, to visit him a few times after the war. The men would go off by themselves and talk, which gave him the opportunity to vent the memories. It was during the first of these visits, that Baughman told Helen about the incident involving Johnny Ryan. Even so, it was forty years after the war before she and her husband were able to talk about it. Henry Fonner died just a few weeks short of his eighty-second birthday, on 21 March 1995. At his funeral, during the graveside service at Oakmount Cemetery, his grandson, David Fonner, who was on leave from the Navy, attended in uniform. His son-in-law, George Blystone, was a pallbearer dressed in the Civil War uniform that he wore for his wedding to Henry's oldest daughter, Ann. Out of respect for his service in World War II, his casket was draped by an American flag and military rites were performed by VFW Post 4793, James Farrell American Legion Post 330, and DAV Post 123, all located in Waynesburg, Pennsylvania. As taps were played, and with his grandson standing at attention and giving him a military salute, this citizen soldier and veteran of the Ardennes Forest in Belgium, was laid to his final rest.

Fred Fonner and Eleanor (Penn) Fonner

Albert Edward Fonner and Annie (Simpson) Fonner

Henry B. Fonner (seated)
And Robert Auld

Sgt. Luther Baughman and Henry B. Fonner

Fonner School on Fonner Run

Greene County, Pennsylvania, is geologically marked by various hills, ridges, valleys, ravines, creeks, and runs. A cursory look at any map shows a myriad of names for these geological features. As one might expect, most of these names have their origins in local native-American lore and family nomenclature of the region's early European explorers and settlers. The name of the Monongahela River, the county's eastern boundary, originated from an old Unami Lenape word meaning "falling banks," referring to the tendency of the river's muddy banks to collapse. Ten Mile Creek got its name from the observation that the mouth of the creek is located ten miles upstream from the early Monongahela River settlement at Fort Redstone (Brownsville). A traveler going upstream on the Ten Mile soon came to a fork in the creek, one to the north and one to the south. The South Branch of Ten Mile Creek could be used to reach an early Greene County settlement, actually in an area whose ownership was disputed by the colonies of Virginia and Pennsylvania, known as Fort Jackson. Until 1796, the land of Greene County was governed as part of Augusta County, Virginia, and later Washington County, Pennsylvania. Settlers moving northwestward from Fort Jackson made their way up the valley of Brown's Creek, near the present intersection of PA Route 18 North and PA Route 21 West. The headwaters of Browns Creek is somewhere on the dividing ridge between Greene and Washington Counties. Before reaching its rendezvous with the South Branch of Ten Mile Creek, however, near the present site of the village of Sycamore, Browns Creek accepts drainage waters from the valley of the Bates Fork Creek. This stream in turns drains numerous ravines, hollows, and narrow vales in northeastern Washington and Morris townships of Greene County. Just northeast of Swarts, across the township line separating Washington and Morris, Bates Fork Creek accepts the waters of a small stream and narrow hollow named Fonner Run.

The earliest record of the Fonner family in Greene County, PA, is 1804 when two brothers, Henry Fonner and William Fonner, brought their families into the region and settled in Morgan (now Washington) Township and Morris Township. Although there are few records, it is known that William Fonner appears as head of his household on the census of 1800 in Bloom Township, Northumberland County, Pennsylvania, not far from Sunbury. The Fonner family was Pennsylvania Dutch in origin. A Henry Fawner appears on a Lancaster County tax roll from 1740. It is not known if he was any relation to the Fonner brothers from Northumberland County. A passenger list of the ship "Richard and Mary", landing in Philadelphia in 1753, suggests that the original German spelling of the Fonner name is "Pfanner." One of the passengers on the ship, Johann Matheis Pfanner, has his name listed as Mathias Fonner on an English list of the foreign passengers' names. The spelling makes sense because in German, a "pfanner" is someone whose trade is gathering salt from boiling down seawater in a large pan. It can also be translated as a tradesman who repairs pans. Family legend indicates an origin in the Rhineland of Germany, so it could be that the salt marshes provided them with at least part of their livelihood. It has been suggested that the Northumberland County Fonners came into Pennsylvania from New Jersey— perhaps Hunterdon County, where several Fonners appear on a militia roll from the Revolutionary period. One of the brothers, William Fonner, is listed as a resident of Somerset County, New Jersey, in a 1788 state census.

William Fonner, and his first wife, Catherine, purchased land near the Lone Oak Church, on Ruff's Creek, Morgan Township (now Washington Township), Greene County, Pennsylvania, from George Huffman on 2 June 1804. In 1805, William and Catherine, both signing the deed, sold their Ruff's Creek property to Jacob Johns. In 1810, William's brother, Henry Fonner, and his wife, appear on the census as residing in Morris Township. After that, there is no further record of Henry Fonner's family in Greene County. William Fonner and his family are also on the 1810 census. By that time, William and Catherine were over forty-five years old and still living in

Morgan Township. Fonner Run received the origin of its name on 1 August 1820, when William Fonner purchased, from Luke Walpole, a tract of land in Morris Township, on a small stream, and a tributary, running into the Bates Fork Creek.

Purchased primarily as farming land for his family, William and his descendants on Fonner Run prospered as farmers for over a century. The hollow as it branched north of the mouth of the run on Bates Fork Creek, provided timber and plenty of water from the stream and numerous springs that fed it. Bottom land, a premium in any hilly farm country, was abundant. The ridges provided good ground for standing timber for building, fencing, and winter heating fuel. There was plenty of game, such as deer, rabbits, squirrels, and birds, of all kinds. As the gentle slopes on the eastern side of the hollow were cleared, fields for corn, hay, gardens, and homesteads were uncovered. In addition, there were neighbors who could help clear those slopes, build fences, and share in the work. The 1820 census revealed that the Fonners' neighbors included Silas Clark, John Hair, Isaac Oaks, and Amos Dyal. William and Catherine Fonner's children over the years cemented lifetime ties to some of the families in the region. Their son, Henry Fonner, no doubt named for his uncle, born somewhere east of Greene County in 1788, married Abigail, the daughter of George and Margaret (Wolverton) Taylor from across the Dividing Ridge in Washington County. The couple established themselves on land in Richhill Township, where they eventually died and were buried in the "Fonner Cemetery" near Bristoria. Another brother of Henry's, Ryaneer Fonner married a woman named Margaret and also lived and worked as a farmer in Richhill Township.   William's youngest son, John Fonner, married into the Conger family.

The Fonners developed their strongest ties, however, with the Frederick Loughman family of Morris Township, early settlers and promoters of the community of West Union. Frederick Loughman was a farmer, blacksmith, and wagon maker. Born in Maryland, Frederick Loughman and his wife, Catherine (Hammers) Loughman, migrated to Greene County prior to 1800, probably about 1797, where they established themselves in northeastern Morris Township. Loughman was a good businessman. He and his first wife, Catherine, were early members of the Presbyterian Church in the area. In the 1830s, the Loughmans joined with fellow Presbyterians in Morris Townships in Washington and Greene County to ask for the establishment of a Cumberland Presbyterian Church in West Union. The Cumberland Presbyterian Church was organized in 1831, and Frederick Loughman donated land and sandstone for construction of the church building, hitching ground, and cemetery. Construction of the stone church was completed in 1833, and the deed from Frederick and Catherine Loughman to the church trustees was finalized in 1840. The West Union congregation was the first Cumberland Presbyterian Church in Pennsylvania.

James Fonner, William and Catherine Fonner's son, born in Pennsylvania in 1794, married Frederick Loughman's daughter, Elizabeth, who had been born around 1798. Elizabeth's brother, David Loughman, married James Fonner's sister, Christena Fonner, who had been born in 1800. The two Morris Township families, therefore, became inextricably enmeshed, and prospered together. In the meantime, Catherine Fonner died, and William Fonner and his second wife, Sarah, by deed dated 23 October 1826, conveyed a portion of the original Fonner Run tract to their neighbor, Isaac Oaks. That same year, William and Sarah Fonner conveyed the remaining portion of the farm on Fonner Run to James Fonner. James and Elizabeth (Loughman) Fonner, spent their entire married life on Fonner Run. They had nine children. James Fonner became a community leader in Morris Township, and was known as a most successful farmer and sheep raiser. At that time, the original family homestead consisted of a log house that stood on the eastern hillside of the small stream running into Fonner Run now designated by the 911 system as Brooks Hollow. Later the family referred to the hillside pasture as the horsefield. In the bottom pasture below, sheep roamed freely, occasionally being sheltered in a wooden structure known as the "Sheep Shed." Until the advent of the 911 system, the entire hollow, including the northeast branch, from Bates Fork Creek past the first fork in Fonner Run to Dividing Ridge in the north and West Union

Hill to the northwest was designated by local residents as Fonner Run.

On 14 October 1864, the "Waynesburg Messenger," noted that James Fonner had assisted in running a Morris Township Democratic Party meeting in Nineveh. The family was pacifist during the Civil War. James' son, Fred Fonner, was exempted from the Pennsylvania state military draft in 1862. The "Sheep Shed" on the farm was the site of a family legend. During the war, one of James' daughters, whose name has been lost in the legend, hid her fiancé in the sheep shed to keep him safe from patrols looking for military draft dodgers and deserters. So far as the legend goes, he remained safe in the shed until the government agents left that part of Morris Township. Despite the war south of the Mason-Dixon line, or maybe as a result, Greene County farmers flourished in the middle to late 19th century. One modern historian of Greene County, Marie Elaine Powell, designates the years 1860 to 1919 as "The Age of Agriculture." By the time of publication of Samuel Bates' *History of Greene County*, in 1888, Ms. Powell notes there were nearly three thousand farms in Greene County encompassing about 361,000 acres, or 98% of the county's land area. The farms were a combination of livestock farms, especially sheep, and food crops such as corn, vegetables, and fruits. As a matter of fact, in 1860, there were twice as many sheep in Greene County than people.

James Fonner and his children on Fonner Run were no exception to this agricultural growth and wealth. Over the years, the original Fonner tract of land was broken up to provide farmsteads to several of the boys and as dowries for the girls. In the meantime, James acquired additional lands from his neighbors. His sons also learned to better themselves by purchasing land, and the deed indexes tell an interesting story. Upon James Fonner's death in 1874, his remaining land was conveyed to his heirs. Frederick Fonner, born on Fonner Run in 1831, took possession of the portion of the farm that contained the original homestead. He continued to raise sheep, improve the ground for crops and hay, cut timber, and with his wife, Eleanor (Penn) Fonner, rear a large brood of sixteen children.

His brother, Phillip Fonner, owned 230 acres of land near the first fork of Fonner Run, and another brother, William Fonner, had possession of over 300 acres up the main branch of Fonner Run near the intersection of a road leading over the hill to West Union.

It is probable that the early Fonners, especially with their German and Pennsylvania Dutch origins, were Baptists. There was a Baptist meeting house and cemetery at the mouth of Fonner Run when William Fonner purchased his land in 1820. Known as the Old Bates Fork Baptist Church, the location is marked on J.L. McConnell's 1865 map of Greene County, Pennsylvania, and the cemetery is clearly shown on the "Caldwell Atlas" 1876 map of Morris Township. There is evidence that the Old Bates Fork Baptist Church congregation was formed as early as the American Revolutionary period and often heard preaching by Reverend John Corbly from Garard's Fort on Muddy Creek. The assembly eventually became a part of the Redstone Baptist Association, and the minutes for the annual meeting of the association in 1808 lists the church as "Bateses Fork Ten Mile." The congregation was represented at the meeting at Uniontown, 22 September 1808 through 25 September 1808, by Michael Cox, John Shideler, and Benjamin Headley. By that year, there were forty-two members. In 1814, the church reported to the Redstone Baptist Association a membership of thirty-one being shepherded by a licensed Baptist preacher, William Stone. The decrease can probably be attributed to the formation of a Baptist congregations in nearby villages and neighboring townships. By 1821, the congregation had declined to twenty-three, but employed an ordained minister, Reverend Ezra DeGarmo. In addition to Reverend DeGarmo, the church was represented at the Redstone Association meeting in Ruff Creek by Elisha Meeks and Nathan Pettit. The minutes record that a "Circular Meeting" was to be held at "Baits" on the Saturday before the third Lord's Day in October, to be attended by representatives of the association, Reverends J. Patton and Mathias Luse. In 1844, the church meeting house stood on lands belonging to John Pettit and Charles Pettit. At that time, 25 March 1844, the Pettits and their wives conveyed the tract of land where the meeting house already stood to the congregation. There is no record of William Fonner's burial site or that of his two wives, but James Fonner, his wife Elizabeth Loughman Fonner, and their unmarried daughter, Jane Fonner, are all buried in well-marked graves in the Old Bates Fork Baptist Cemetery on Fonner Run. In January 1871, the Bates Fork Baptist Church was granted a parcel of land by Thomas W. Taylor in Washington Township, and the congregation built and moved to a new church building in Sycamore, Pennsylvania.

At least three of James Fonner's sons continued to grow and prosper as farmers after his death. William Fonner, Phillip Fonner, and Fred Fonner, owned about a thousand acres of Fonner Run among their individual farms. Fred Fonner's granddaughter, Golda B. (Fonner) Auld, remembered, in a 1976 interview, that when she was a little girl, about 1400 acres in the hollow were owned by various members of the family. By 1876, William Fonner had a large interest in sheep. As a farmer and wool grower, he was listed in "Caldwell's Atlas" as owning four hundred sheep on four hundred seventy acres. His brother, Fred, ran two hundred sheep on three hundred acres. Phillip Fonner, with two hundred thirty acres, sold wool from two hundred sheep, and Goldie Auld recalled that he and his wife at one time had ninety-nine turkeys. In addition, Phillip also was involved in cutting and selling timber. James Fonner had a saw mill in 1865, and no doubt the mill contributed cut timbers and rough cut boards for the barns, sheds, chicken houses, and various outbuildings that dotted the hollow. The log homestead was replaced by clapboard, framed, farm houses with sealed tin roofs. Eventually, as time went on, split-rail fences were replaced by modern wire and barbed wire fences strung and attached to sturdy posts of locust wood. Goldie Auld and her sister, Grace (Fonner) Rinehart, remembered the farms as showplaces. Between the end of the Civil War and World War I, the Fonner families on Fonner Run were "very prosperous," related Goldie, and "had everything they ever wanted." The farms were doing quite well. When Goldie and Grace were girls, thirty cents per pound was a good price for wool. Each of the farms had cows, horses, pigs, chickens, and lots of sheep. The girls often saw turkeys, cattle, and pigs being driven down the road to market. The farmers would fatten chickens and turkeys to sell in the winter. The families' larders were well stocked with canned beans, potatoes, pickles, relish, and all kinds of fruits from the peach orchards, apple orchards, and pear trees. There were numerous berry bushes, and some farms even had grape arbors. A few, like Fred Fonner's farm, even had ponds stocked with fish.

William Fonner and Phillip Fonner had a sugar camp. A hired man named Mr. Gray would boil down the sap taken from the numerous maple trees. One room was full of molasses. Goldie remembered that her grandfather usually employed a hired hand, and one picture of Fred Fonner taken in front of his house with four of his daughters and his son, Albert, also has an unidentified hired hand standing next to Fred in the photograph. Hired help usually made $15 or $17 per month. Once the W&W Railroad was constructed, it was common for the families to make a trip into Waynesburg about once a month to conduct business and do a little shopping. Goldie's brother, Henry B. Fonner, told about taking the train into Waynesburg with his parents, Albert Fonner and Annie (Simpson) Fonner. While in town he was permitted to buy one bag of penny candy. The candy would then last him until the next month's trip on the train. Usually the family would walk to Swarts Station to board the train. Goldie said that they would generally catch the train at 10:00 A.M. and come back from town on the 3:00 P.M. run. The fare from Swarts was forty cents for a round trip to Waynesburg and back. In addition to farming and raising sheep, Fred Fonner had a passion for fox hunting. He had a pair of prized fox hounds. He was proud of the dogs and showed his pride by having their picture painted on the side of his barn. Before he died, Fred Fonner deeded about ninety acres of land along with a farmhouse and tenant house to his son Albert E. Fonner. The remainder of his farm he granted in his Will to his four unmarried daughters, each girl to have an equal share until she got married, at which time her share would go to be divided among the other sisters. Two of the girls eventually married, and the farm remained in the hands of the twin sisters, Myrtle and Emma Fonner, until their deaths. All in all, Goldie and Grace had pleasant memories of their girlhood life on Fonner

Run.

William Fonner, Sr., and his wife Catherine were both literate, and education was important to the Fonners from the earliest times. About the time of James Fonner's death in 1874, or perhaps a few years earlier, the Fonner family set aside a small parcel of James Fonner's land, near the southwest corner of a hayfield, located a few yards up the first fork in the road on Fonner Run, to be used for a one-room schoolhouse. A framed and clapboard building, with a tin roof, was erected and a small spring which opened on the roadside below the school was improved to provide water for the students. The Fonner School is marked on the Caldwell Atlas map of Morris Township. Generations of Fonner children, as well as their neighbors, attended school there for up to eight grades. High school education could be obtained in Nineveh at the Morris Township high school. Albert Fonner, son of Fred Fonner, had several children who attended the school, and two daughters, Goldie (Fonner) Auld and Georgie (Fonner) Lewis, taught there for short periods. In 1905, the teacher at the school, Olma M. Loughman, published a report for the school's activities for the month of November. There were twenty-three students in the school, ten boys and thirteen girls. Average attendance was ninety-one percent. Students with perfect attendance included Ruth Thompson, Georgia Fonner, Nora Petit, Ethel Petit, Fred Thompson, David Kearns, and James Kearns. Those missing two days or less were Alma Brooks, Dora Pettit, and Hettie Fonner. Georgia and Hettie were Albert Fonner's children, and the school was located on the edge of his hayfield. The teacher invited any interested parties to attend the school's Literary Society meeting on 21 December 1905. Over the years, the Morris Township school directors provided various teachers. Among these was a Mrs. Malady, who taught school when it was attended by Albert's youngest son, Henry B. Fonner, and Henry's nephew, Robert Auld. Years later, in 1966, Mrs. Malady was a long-term substitute teacher for fourth grade at the Nineveh elementary school, and one of her students was Henry's son, Kent Fonner. She delighted in telling Kent what a good student his father had been when he was a boy. Another teacher at the school was Web Black from Nineveh, who also taught Henry's oldest son, Bryan, for first through third grades at the Nineveh school in the 1950s. Bryan remembers best the nature hikes that Mr. Black would take with his students and the hot dog roast held on the last day of each school year. The Fonner School was in operation from at least the 1870s for about 60 or 70 years, until elementary students in Morris Township were sent to a large, more modern school in Nineveh.

Fonner Run's relative isolated and rural environment was shattered in 1897 with the discovery of oil on the William Fonner farm and the development of the Fonner oil field. Called "the biggest strike ever made in Greene County," the Fonner No. 1 oil well came into production March 1897 near the intersection of Fonner Run Road and the road to West Union. The well was a gusher with a six inch stream that sent crude oil running down the creek by the barrel. Initially producing five hundred barrels a day, eventually the well produced as much as 1800 barrels per day for a short time and then declined. The well was drilled by Timothy Ross from West Union down to a depth of 2700 feet when he struck a large pool of oil. As a wildcatter operating in Morris Township, Ross drilled many dry holes before bringing in the Fonner gusher. The well was a joint venture of Ross's Morris Township Oil Company and the Carnegie Gas Company. It was reported in newspapers that Ross and the Carnegie field superintendent had made an agreement to drill the well on the Fonner farm if McKinley was elected president in 1896. The agreement specified that if oil was found, then the well belonged to Ross and his investors. If the well produced gas, then it belonged to Carnegie.

Investors in the Morris Township Oil Company included James Dunn, Joseph Dunn, William Fonner, John M. Dunn, and A. B. Reese. Another benefactor from the well was C. H. Bowlby, who had a one-eighth interest in the William Fonner lease. Within a week after the strike, it was reported that all the farms between Waynesburg and the William Fonner property had been leased. Phillip Fonner, who owned the farm just a mile south of the well, received a $5000 bonus for a lease on his farm. The South Penn Oil Company bought the Fonner No. 1 well on 30 April 1897, paying a sum of $223,000 to the Morris

One of the last wells on the Fonner Oil Field

Township Oil Company and the Farmers Oil Company as the purchase price. In the meantime, Ross drilled another gusher on the Bristor farm, five hundred feet North of the Fonner No. 1 well. The field generated such excitement that dignitaries from Standard Oil inspected the Fonner well in may 1897, arriving in Dunn Station by train and taking carriages to the Fonner field. Other wells were successful in the Fonner field on the Brooks and Shoup farms. Still another belt of producing wells was later drilled on the ridge between Ruff Creek and Bates Fork Creek in Washington Township. This extension of the Fonner field was an area two miles long with producing wells on the Huffman, Meeks, and Closser farms. By 1932, the Fonner field had about fifty producing wells and the oil was piped to a tank yard at Meadowlands in Washington County.

In August 1897, William Fonner was interviewed by a newspaper reporter from Pittsburgh. At that time, the Fonner well was producing 800 barrels a day. Calling him "lucky Bill" Fonner, the reporter interviewed him in his cornfield. Newspapermen found him to be a "bluff old farmer," who still tended his 700 sheep. It was reported that he was making $120 a day from the oil being produced from his land. This seemed a tremendous return on his initial investment of $450 into a one-eighth interest in the well. At that time, he said that he had no real need for all the money and seemed uncomfortable with the publicity coming his way. Still, Fonner was considered a wealthy man by his neighbors and the rest of his family. Throughout it all, however, the money from the well did not seem to change him much. Goldie Auld and Grace Rinehart remembered that their great uncle Bill Fonner was a hard man to get along with before they found oil on his farm and he remained "contrary" even after the oil came in. So as far as they could tell, the oil made no difference in his attitude toward the rest of the family. His example, however, set the whole region buzzing with excitement.

After the Fonner well came in, people in the area were excited, and Goldie remembered that everyone wondered if they might have oil too. "It was an exciting place for a while," she said, with quite a lot of drilling around and quite a lot of wells.

A well was drilled on the Phillip Fonner farm. All they found was "a little gas, but it didn't amount to anything – – so it was dry too." She remembered other wells on the Loughman property near West Union and that Lincoln Dunn had wells at Dunn Station. Her comments about some of the families who found oil on their farms were quite interesting. She said that it was "quite a time" when an oil well was drilled on the Wright family farm. She remembered that Mr. Wright was poor, and it helped him out when the well came in. She also said the Meeks family, when they found oil in their farm, were also "very worthy of it." She thought the last will drilled in the Fonner field was the Wright well.

Both Goldie and Grace talked about the family's experience when a well was drilled on Fred Fonner's land, just east of the William Fonner farm. The well came in dry. "We didn't get anything in the well," Goldie remembered, but the experience and excitement of having a well drilled stayed with them both throughout their lives. The contractors for the well were two men named Sellers and Ogden, both very nice men, "very much businessmen." The drillers and tool dressers all boarded with the family on the farm. They remembered that like anyone else, some the men were "all right and some weren't." Mr. Blackburn and Harry Gray were two oil drillers who boarded on the Fred Fonner farm. Goldie's young son, Robert Auld, and her younger brother, Henry B. Fonner, were so impressed by the two that they began playing that they were oil drillers too. Two other well workers, Dick Hughes and Raymond Black, also stayed with the family. All of them were decent men. There was one other man, however, whose named they did not remember, who was said to "drink some." Throughout the drilling operation, they all got along nicely and the workers became like family.

Of course all the equipment to the well had to be hauled into the site by horses. Grace Rinehart was certain that Frank Petit from Ruff Creek did some of the hauling. He used his own horses and wagons to bring in the equipment. As she said, it "took an awful lot [of] things." Goldie was impressed by one thing regarding the hauling of equipment into the well site.

"My, the mud they'd have to go through," she exclaimed," My!" Even though the well came in dry, they noted that one nice thing about it was that they all got to see the drilling crew at work. The whole family found it quite interesting to watch the engine, band wheel, walking beam and derrick in operation. They were especially impressed by the labor involved in dressing the tools.

When the wells dried up in the Fonner field, each well was plugged and the casing was pulled. The Fonner No. 1 well was still pumping oil into the late 1960s or early 1970s. Albert Fonner's older sons, Jim and Hugh Fonner, worked on the casing crews when the casing was pulled from the wells. For some reason, casing was always pulled at night, so working on the casing crews still left the boys time to do some work around the farm during the day. When asked how people in the area reacted when the wells began to be plugged and abandoned, Goldie and Grace said that of course people would be disappointed, especially if they were getting free gas from the wells under their farm. All in all, though, the people around the Fonner field seem to have taken a stoic attitude toward the situation. Having experienced a run of good fortune when successful wells were drilled, neither heard their friends and neighbors say very much about it when the wells were gone.

The last Fonner family to live and farm on Fonner Run was Henry B. Fonner and his wife, Helen (Jacobs) Fonner, and their six children. Henry was a grandson of Fred Fonner and the youngest child of Albert E. Fonner and Annie (Simpson) Fonner. He was born on his parents' farm in 1913 at about the same time as his nephew, Robert Auld, Goldie (Fonner) Auld's son. Robert's father had been killed in a farming accident, and he and his mother lived in the tenant house on the Albert Fonner place. The boys were like brothers and grew together. The family tells a story about when they were quite young. Robert got a new pair of shoes. He left them in the main house one night when he went home to the nearby tenant house. Coming back" for his shoes, he found his uncle Henry wearing them and stomping around the house, with apparent delight. Robert looked and asked, "who's shoes are those Henry dear?"

During the excitement when oil and gas wells were being drilled on Fonner Run, the boys played that they were drilling wells too. Henry was Harry Gray, and Robert was Mr. Blackburn, the names of two drillers who worked in the Fonner oilfield. Goldie said they called themselves Blackburn and Gray so much, she thought they changed their names. One of the neighbors told the widowed mother that a boy needed to learn to handle a gun, so when they were nine or ten, she bought a rifle and allowed them to take it and go hunting on the farm. She would hand the weapon to them out of a back window of her house, and they would hand it back in when they were done. While the boys grew, the 20th century impinged on Fonner Run. When the first airplane flew over the farm, the boys ran around excited and whooped and hollered with delight. Model A and Model T Ford automobiles replaced road wagons and buggies on the roads in the hollow. Henry's brother, Hugh Fonner, bought a Model T and gave the boys rides on the back country roads. When Henry and Robert were sixteen, they got their own car. Once, when Henry was driving his sister, Goldie, and his niece, Virginia Bell Lewis, to town, he somehow ran off the road and down the bank into a pasture near the mouth of Fonner Run known as Huffman's field. He drove the vehicle down the pasteur and through a gate back onto the road, but Virginia Bell declared, "No more ridin' with Henry!"

While his brothers all left the farm for jobs in other parts of Western Pennsylvania and Ohio, Henry stayed to help his parents keep things going. The golden age for the farm was already fading. A severe epidemic of foot rot made the bottom pasture unfit for sheep. The disease stays in the ground for decades. The family continued to survive on the land, but the years of prosperity were slipping away. Annie Fonner died in 1940, and when Henry was drafted into the Army in November 1942, his father became convinced that his son was not coming back from the war. He eventually sickened and died in July 1944, having given up the will to live.

Henry Fonner building a haystack,

In later years pumping gasoline into a tank truck.

Henry and his wife returned to the farm after he came back from service in World War II. In 1946, his brothers and sisters deeded the farm to him as part of the settlement of Albert Fonner's estate. By that time, however, it was clear that farming on Fonner run could not be more than subsistence. Land provided the family with food and shelter, but Henry, in addition to farming, also worked for twenty-five years as a warehouseman and laborer for Jacobs Oil Products, later Jacobs Petroleum Products, Inc., in Waynesburg. He could often be seen at the Jacobs bulk plant unloading or loading tank trucks, or on the road in a utility truck delivering kerosene or heating fuel in cans to Jacobs' customers. In addition, his wife Helen worked various jobs at the sewing factories in Waynesburg and eventually retired as an extension nutrition aid for Penn State.

The Fonner children, however, have warm memories of life on the farm. Milking cows, feeding livestock, gathering eggs, haying in the summer, and working in the gardens instilled values and appreciation for hard work. Henry Fonner's oldest son, Bryan, remembers an early lesson he learned from his father while they were working in the garden one evening. Some neighbors were walking by on the road. They were extremely poverty-ridden, and the boys had a reputation in the neighborhood for being bullies and thieves. As they neared the place where Bryan and his father were working, his father stopped and stood to talk with the walkers for a few minutes. After their neighbors moved on down the road, Bryan remembers his Dad telling him, "Everyone deserves some respect, no matter what their reputation or how you might feel about them." A few years later, when Bryan was in high school, he heard some of the old neighbor boys talking. They were telling someone how when they were kids they stole from everybody up the hollow on Fonner Run except "Old Man Fonner," because he always treated them right.

Like generations before him, Henry Fonner farmed using a team of horses. Over the years he had several different matched pairs, and he was quite skilled as a horseman. As Bryan grew, he acquired his father's skill with driving a team of Belgians through the gardens or across the hayfield. At that time, the Fonners still cut, raked, and shocked the hay before it was picked up on a horse-drawn hay wagon or sled. The work was often done by Henry, his son, Bryan, and his daughter, Ellen. Sometimes a neighbor boy or one or two of the kids' cousins lent a hand. Bryan and Ellen became skilled at lifting a shock of hay onto the load as their father properly stacked it so it did not fall off on the trip to the barn. At the barn, the hay was thrown up into the mow, and the kids stacked it for storage. Sometimes, the family still built haystacks in the field. The last team of horses they used was a big, gentle pair of Belgians named Kit and Bird. Bryan became the first Fonner on Fonner Run to farm with a tractor when, at the age of sixteen, he purchased a used Farmall Super C tractor and a set of plows with money he earned working for the summer on his Uncle Ben Jacobs' farm near Jefferson. A final end to the farm, however, came when the farmhouse burned in January 1967. Shortly thereafter the farm was sold, and the family lived in Nineveh, and then Deerlick, before Henry and Helen Fonner moved to Waynesburg with their three youngest children, and eventually retired. The last Fonner to own land on Fonner Run, Henry's son, Kent Fonner, sold his parcel of 19.11 acres that he had purchased in 1980 in 1994, when he moved with his family and took a job in Northeast Pennsylvania.

Since the 1960s, the landscape of Fonner Run has started to revert to its natural state. Woods once cleared by Fonner ancestors are encroaching on the pastures and fields improved for livestock and crops. There are still residents in the hollow, but none of them are Fonners. The barns, sheds, and outbuildings built by earlier families have disappeared. Many of the clapboard farmhouse built after the Civil War are also gone and have been replaced by modern split-level homes, double-widetrailers, and hunting cabins. The site of the old Fonner School is grown over with brush and trees, and the remains of the spring along the roadside have become difficult to locate. The oil derricks on the Fonner oilfield were removed recently during the present oil and gas exploration being done in Greene County for fracking purposes. There does not appear to be much farming in the hollow. Instead, one family has established a private game farm and preserve for hunting purposes. Fonner

Run still flows from the headwaters of the Dividing Ridge and West Union Hill down to Bates Fork Creek. The old Baptist Church was long ago moved to Sycamore, but the cemetery remains as a monument to those early Baptists who established themselves as a congregation at the mouth of Fonner Run. Those early residents who are buried there, including Fonner ancestors, James Fonner, Elizabeth Fonner, and their daughter Jane, remain silent witnesses and sentinels to the hollow which they once called home. The ground and creeks remain, markers of a distant past and harbingers of a future for the next generation and beyond.

Henry B. Fonner on the farm with a scythe.

CHAPTER III
FONNER FAMILY NOTES

William Fonner appears on the 1800 census as head of his family in Bloom Township, Northumberland County, PA [The county seat is Sunbury. Since 1800, Bloom Township is now part of Columbia County, PA, and I believe is part of the town of Bloomsburg.] Dorothy Hennen believed that the Fonners originally settled in New Jersey. I believe the original German spelling for our name was "Pfanner." It comes from the German word for "pan," and may refer to someone who repairs pans, like a tinsmith, or I also found a definition indicating that a "pfanner" was someone who boiled down seawater for salt, as in a pan. There is still research to do in this area.

William Fonner and his brother, Henry, migrated to Greene County, PA, sometime between 1800 and 1804. On 2 June 1804, William and his wife, Catherine, purchased land on Ruff's Creek from George Huffman. In 1805, they sold the Ruff Creek property to Jacob Johns. In 1810, the family appears on the census for Morgan Township [a part of which became Washington Twp]. On 1 August 1820, William Fonner purchased a tract of land in Morris Twp, Greene County, PA, near the Bates Fork Branch of Ten Mile Creek, from Luke Walpole. In 1826, William Fonner and his second wife, Sarah, conveyed a portion of his land to Isaac Oaks (10/23/1826) and a portion to James Fonner. William signed his name to the deed, and Sarah made her mark.

WILLIAM FONNER (parents?) b. prior to 1765; died Morris Twp, Greene County, PA, after 1826; married (1) Catherine, b. prior to 1765, died Greene County, PA, between 1805 and 1810, (2) Sarah. Children of William and Catherine Fonner:

1.   Henry Fonner m. Abigail Taylor

2. James Fonner m. Elizabeth Loughman*
3. Christina Fonner m. David Loughman, brother of Elizabeth Loughman
4. Ryaneer Fonner m. Margaret
5. John Fonner m. a Conger

*JAMES FONNER, b. in PA in 1794; died Morris Twp, Greene County, PA, 3/19/1874, age 80 yrs and 25 days; married Elizabeth Loughman, daughter of Frederick and Catherine Loughman [Frederick's father, according to Loughman family papers, may have been a Frederick Loughman, Senior, who was reported to be a Revolutionary War veteran], b. in PA about 1798; died Morris Twp, Greene County, PA, 6/25/1866, age 67 yrs. Both are buried along with their daughter Jane in old Bates Fork Baptist Cemetery on Fonner Run near Swartz, PA. Children:

1. Lucinda Fonner m. Richard Iams
2. Christina Fonner m. Samuel Moniger
3. Eva Fonner m. (1) Hedge (2) John McCullough
4. William Fonner m. Jane
5. Frederick Fonner m. Eleanor Penn*
6. James Fonner, Jr., m. Eliza Taylor
7. Philip Fonner m. Letitia
8. Elizabeth Fonner m. Samuel McCorrel
9. Jane Fonner (never married)

*FREDERICK FONNER, b. 1831 in Morris Twp, Greene County, PA; died 6/25/1906; m. Eleanor Penn. Children:

1. John Fonner
2. Frank Fonner
3. Henry Fonner
4. Albert Edward Fonner m. Annie Simpson*
5. Stephen Fonner
6. George Fonner
7. James Fonner
8. Cora Fonner (died of typhoid fever believed carried by oil driller or from fish ponds on Fonner farm)

9.   Myrtle Fonner (twin)
10. Emma Fonner (twin)
11. Jessie Fonner m. Joseph Thompson [children are Emma
     (Babe) and Luther]
12. Elizabeth Fonner m. John Cox
13. Mary
14. Jane
15. And 16. Twin boys who died at birth

*ALBERT EDWARD FONNER, b. 3/1863, Morris Twp, Greene County, PA; died 7/1944; m. Annie Simpson, daughter of Hugh and Esther Patterson Simpson, on 3/30/1890; b. Morris Twp, 1868, died Morris Twp, 1940. Both are buried in West Union Cemetery. On 12/15/1900, Frederick Fonner and Eleanor, his wife, conveyed 91 acres 111perches of land in Morris Twp to Albert Fonner. Children:

1.   Goldie Fonner m. John Auld
2.   Hettie Fonner m. Joseph Dunn
3.   Grace Fonner m. Frederick Rinehart
4.   Blanche Fonner
5.   Georgie Fonner m. Paul Lewis
6.   Hugh Fonner m. Edith Fultz
7.   Mary Fonner m. Isaac Stickles
8.   James Fonner m. Mary
9.   Henry B. Fonner m. Helen Mae Jacobs*